W9-CMG-929

THE GIANT BEAST THAT TERRIFIED ANCIENT HUMANS

By Barbara Hehner / Illustrations by Mark Hallett

Scientific consultation by Dr. Mark Engstrom and Dr. Kevin Seymour

A MADISON PRESS BOOK

produced for

CROWN PUBLISHERS · NEW YORK

WONDERS IN A SECRET CAVE

The favorite hobby of Jean-Marie Chauvet and his two friends was to explore caves in the rugged Ardèche region of southeast France. On a cold, sunny afternoon in December 1994, following an old mule path, they climbed to a ledge partway up a cliff. After squeezing through a narrow opening, they entered a small cave. At its far end, behind some fallen rocks, Jean-Marie could feel a faint current of air. Because they had explored many caves before, the three knew there might be another, bigger cave hidden somewhere behind. They moved the rocks and wriggled through a tunnel, following the draft to a dark passageway below. When they shouted into the hole, their excited voices echoed back for a long time. There must be an enormous chamber below! Though tired from their exertions, the three were full of excitement. What could be down there?

After unrolling their ladder into the passageway, the three friends climbed down, one by one, to the floor of a vast cave with high ceilings. They stood for a moment in the total silence, the inky darkness lit only by the thin beams of light from their helmet lamps. Then they began to move slowly, in single file. On the ground, their lamps picked out thousands of bear bones. On the walls were numerous bear claw scratches. Then one of the explorers gasped in amazement. Her lamp shone on the vivid image of a mammoth, an animal that had been extinct for over 10,000 years.

Soon the three friends saw that the walls of the cave were alive with prehistoric paintings of animals in red and black. The ancient artists had used shading as well as the natural shape of the rocks to round out the animals' bodies, so that they seemed ready to leap off the walls. Many of the animals were large and dangerous — lions, woolly rhinoceroses, and cave bears. The three explorers realized that finding this cave was an extraordinary event. They were the first people in thousands of years to look at this art.

Venturing farther, carefully so as not to touch the walls or disturb the objects on the floors, they found chamber after chamber filled with art. And in one of them, they saw something so strange that they caught their breath. On a large square stone, someone long ago had carefully placed a bear skull. On the floor around it were more bear skulls.

Was this an altar to the cave bear? Had both humans and bears lived in this cave? What did the art mean to the people who had created it by the flickering light of burning torches? Had these ancient humans worshiped the cave bear?

Jean-Marie Chauvet and his two friends look in amazement at the underground chambers later named the Chauvet Cave.

TALES TOLD BY BONES AND TEETH

Even though the last cave bears died out about 10,000 years ago, they left behind many clues to what they looked like and how they lived. Above all, they left us their bones, hundreds of thousands of bones, in caves from France to Belgium, Holland, Germany, and Switzerland, eastward to Poland and south into Spain and Italy.

From these bones, scientists know that cave bears were as big as Kodiak bears, the largest brown bears found in Alaska today. Standing on their hind legs, male cave bears were as much as eight feet (2.4 m) tall. On all fours, they might have been five feet (1.5 m) tall at the shoulder. They weighed up to 1,500 pounds (680 kg). Females were much smaller than the males, perhaps a third to half the size. All cave bears had heavy, barrel-shaped bodies and their legs were short, but thick and powerful.

Cave bears had even larger heads than Kodiak bears, and there was a distinct "step" from their muzzles to their broad, domed foreheads. (This is what makes them easy to recognize when portrayed in cave art.) Their eye sockets were smaller than those of brown bears, but their nasal cavities were very large, suggesting an animal that relied more on a keen sense of smell than on eyesight to locate food.

Because of their enormous size, like large bears today, cave bears would have had few natural enemies.

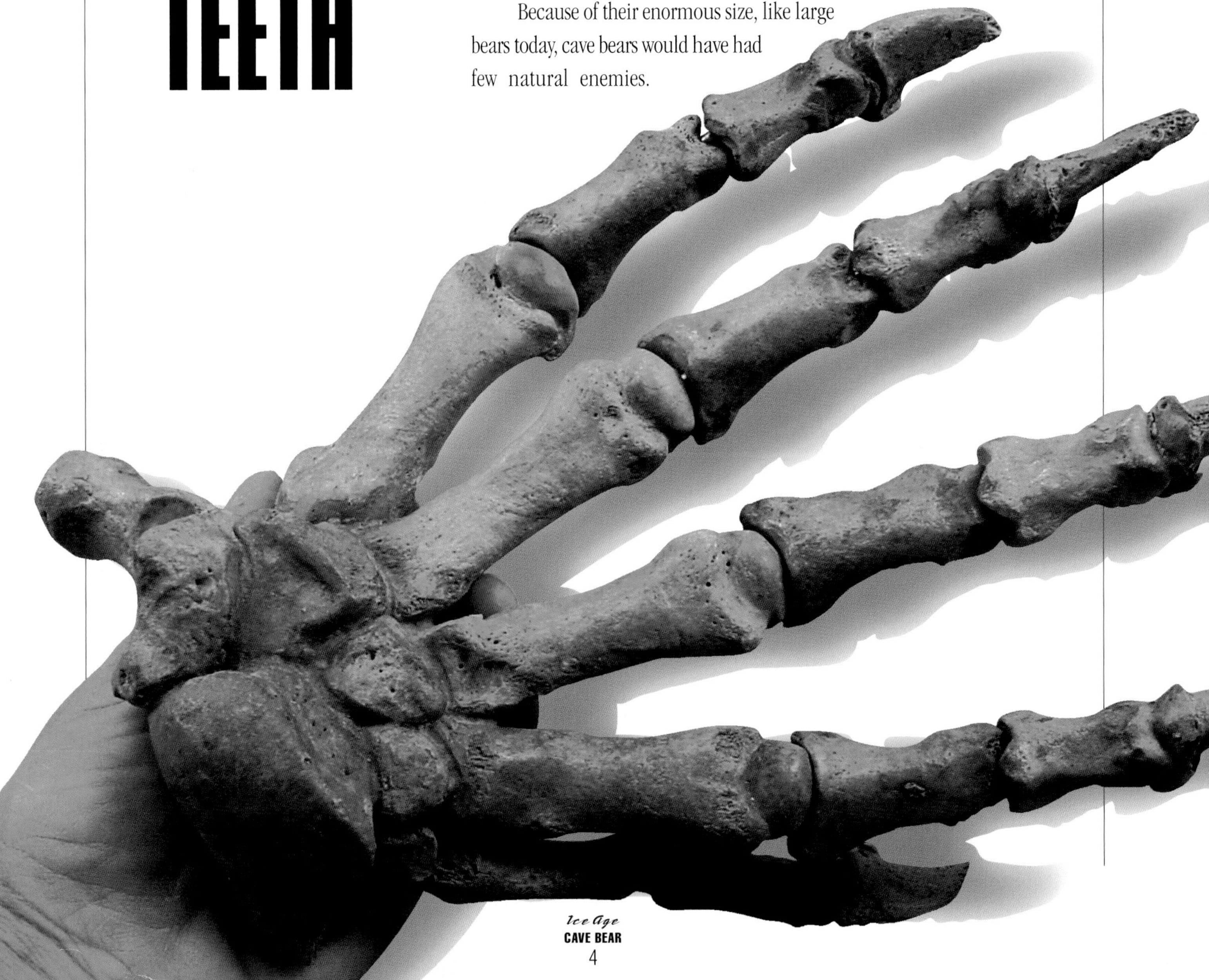

And yet the experts have concluded that for all their massive bodies, long claws, and pointed canine teeth (the fangs on either side of their mouths), cave bears were mostly plant-eaters. The evidence is at the back of their mouths: large grinding molars — much larger than those of today's brown bears — for mashing plants. Raw plant fibers are very hard on teeth. Scientists have found that the molars of old cave bears, those that had lived for 20 years or so, were worn down to stubs.

At different times and places, bears have eaten a wide range of food. The cave bear menu probably consisted of grasses and other plants and berries. The bears may also have enjoyed fish, insects, small animals, and leftovers from lion or hyena kills. Their excellent sense of smell may have helped them locate decaying carcasses just as bears do today.

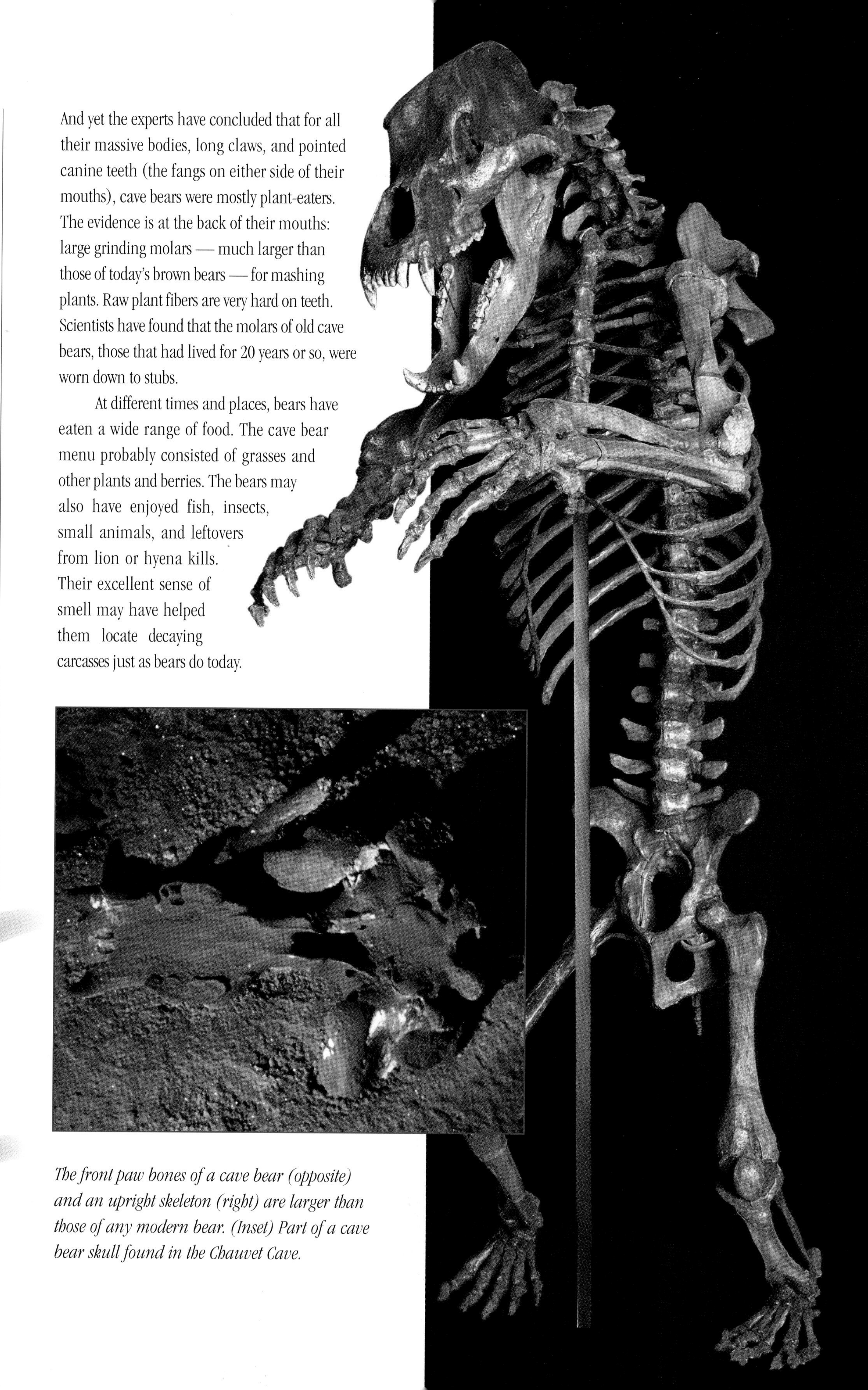

The front paw bones of a cave bear (opposite) and an upright skeleton (right) are larger than those of any modern bear. (Inset) Part of a cave bear skull found in the Chauvet Cave.

PICTURING AN ANCIENT GIANT

How do we know as much as we do about an animal that died out 10,000 years ago? By studying the size and shape of its bones, scientists can reconstruct its muscles and flesh and imagine the cave bear in motion.

Cave bears would have walked with a slow, rolling gait, their feet turned in sharply. They were probably too heavy to climb trees, except perhaps for cubs escaping danger. Like most bears today, they lumbered along using the entire soles of their feet. The heel went down first and then the toes, the same way human beings walk. The bears' long, flat hind feet would support them if they reared upright and took a few steps. Like bears today, cave bears probably stood up to look around and sniff their surroundings.

Cave bear paws were enormous — the paw prints they left behind in caves measure as much as seven inches (18 cm) across. Most modern brown bear prints are only about four inches (10 cm) across. Each bear paw ended in five toes with curved claws, not as long as those of a brown bear but thicker. Strong claws and big front paws came in handy for digging up roots and tubers as well as the nests of small animals. Perhaps cave bears, like some brown bears today, used their paws to swat and kill small rodents which they then ate.

Although prehistoric artists saw living cave bears, they had only red and black paints to work with and drew only the bears' outlines. Scientists therefore have to make educated guesses about what the fur of these creatures was like. Since the bears lived in northern regions in a time when winters were long and cold, they likely had shaggy outer coats like those of Kodiaks, with a soft, fuzzy layer underneath to hold their body heat. What color was their fur? All the brown bears alive today have coats of solid colors — no stripes or spots — ranging from black to cinnamon brown to blond. So cave bears were probably in this color range, too.

COMPARE THIS LIFE-SIZE CAVE BEAR PAW WITH YOUR OWN HAND

Bigger and broader than those of a modern-day brown bear, a cave bear's huge front paws would have been useful for digging up the roots and tubers of plants it liked to eat.

Cave bears had their earliest beginnings in a small mammal called *Miacis*, which lived about 40 to 30 million years ago. Miacis had a long, thin body and looked like a weasel. It may not have appeared very ferocious as it scrambled up a tree, but it had teeth designed for killing. Opening its little mouth in a snarl, it revealed sharp, pointed canine teeth that could pierce flesh. Farther back in its jaw were shearing teeth that could tear off chunks of meat. Miacis was likely the first carnivore (meat-eating mammal), from which all other carnivores descended.

Over the next 15 million years, the carnivores split into different groups — including dogs, cats, hyenas, and seals — but there were still no animals that looked like bears. Instead, there was an odd branch on the dog family tree, a group of animals known as the bear-dogs. One of these, *Cephalogale,* was the size and general shape of a dog, but inside its mouth was something new — not only the cutting teeth of meat-eaters, but flat, grinding teeth for eating plants. From those early times in bear history right to the present day, bears have been able to eat both meat and plants.

DAWN OF THE BEARS

▲ **Miacis**
40–30 million
years ago

▲ **Cephalogale**
30–20 million
years ago

▲ **Ursavus elemensis**
20–18 million
years ago

Cephalogale was probably the ancestor of the first animal that was clearly a bear — *Ursavus elemensis,* the dawn bear. When the dawn bear appeared in Europe some 20 million years ago, the land was covered with subtropical forests. Palm trees grew and crocodiles swam in the rivers. The terrier-sized dawn bear probably lived on insects, small animals, and plants.

Millions of years went by, and the climate became cooler and drier. Bears became larger and spread out through Asia, Africa, and North and South America. Six million years ago, an enormous bear called *Agriotherium africanum* ranged all over Africa. Nearly four times the size of a modern lion, it probably weighed about 1,650 pounds (750 kg). A group of bears called the *tremarctines* occupied North and South America. One of these bears would become the largest bear of the ice age — the short-faced bear.

Meanwhile, in the evergreen forests of Europe lived a bear called *Ursus minimus*. Just as its name suggests, it was small and weighed between 60 and 140 pounds (27 to 64 kg), about the size of the smallest modern bear, the sun bear of Malaysia. But Ursus minimus gave rise to great things: its descendants evolved into cave bears, as well as most of the bears in the world today, including black bears and brown bears. As the Ursus bears slowly became larger, the earth's climate was also going through enormous changes. By the time of the cave bear, *Ursus spelaeus,* the ice age had arrived.

Agriotherium africanum 6–5 million years ago ▶
Short-Faced Bear 1.1 million years ago–10,000 years ago ▼
◀ Spectacled Bear 1 million years ago–present day
Giant Panda 1.3 million years ago–present day ▼
Cave Bear 300,000–10,000 years ago ▼
▼ Ursus minimus 6–5 million years ago
◀ Brown Bear 1 million years ago–present day
◀ Sun Bear 1.7 million years ago–present day
▲ Polar Bear 200,000 years ago–present day
▲ Asiatic Black Bear 2 million years ago–present day
▲ Sloth Bear 1.5 million years ago–present day
American Black Bear 1.6 million years ago–present day ▲

WHAT CAUSES AN ICE AGE?

The earth's climate becomes much cooler during an ice age, and scientists think that this is because of several factors working together over a long period of time. The shifting of the continents and the formation of new mountains could have altered wind and weather patterns, bringing cooler temperatures. Decreasing levels of carbon dioxide in the earth's atmosphere, perhaps from volcanic eruptions, may also have caused global cooling. As a result of changes to the earth's orbit or to the tilt of the earth's axis, less sunlight could have fallen in one hemisphere than in the other. Eventually, huge ice sheets spread across the earth. These vast expanses of white snow and ice would reflect most of the sun's heat back into space, so that less would be absorbed by the earth's surface.

DEEP FREEZE

The earth has existed for about 4.6 billion years. During that vast length of time, its climate has gone through enormous changes. Through most of the age of dinosaurs, from about 200 to 65 million years ago, the earth was much hotter than it is now. It was warm even at the North and South poles, which had no ice caps, even in winter. But at other times, the earth has been much colder than it is today, with ice blanketing up to a third of its surface. The colder periods are called ice ages.

The most recent ice age began about 1.7 million years ago and ended about 10,000 years ago. This time is also known as the *Pleistocene Epoch*. Even during the Pleistocene, there were warmer periods, known as interglacials — but the cold and ice always returned. About 20,000 years ago, ice covered large parts of Europe, Asia, and North America. In Europe, much of the British Isles, all of Scandinavia, and northern Germany were covered by ice. In North America, the ice reached as far south as present-day Missouri and in some places was two miles (3.2 km) thick.

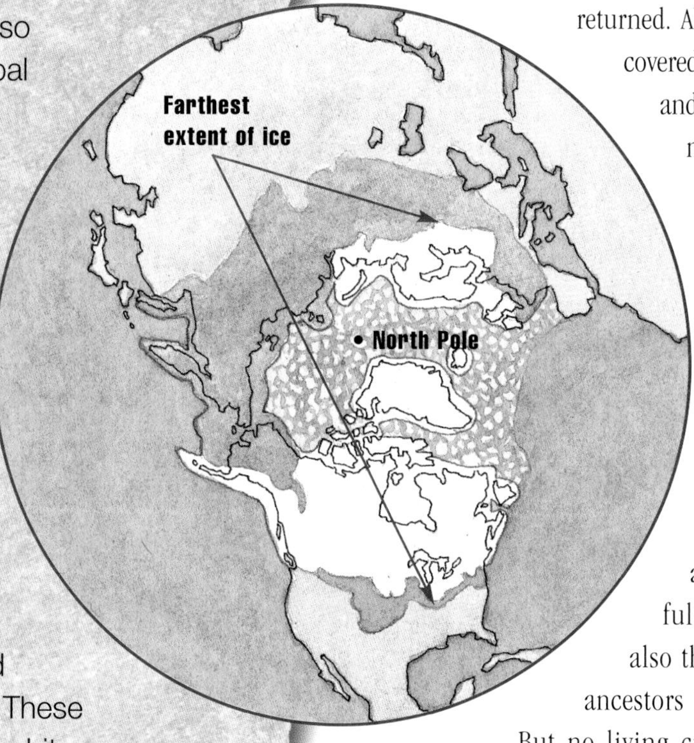

The Pleistocene was a time of rugged, powerfully built mammals. It was also the time when our human ancestors first appeared in Europe. But no living creatures, not even hardy, thick-coated animals like cave bears and woolly mammoths, lived right on the ice sheets. Instead, they lived to the south of the glaciers, on plains and in mountain valleys that were similar to today's subarctic tundra, but with many more plants to eat.

HIBERNATION

When the intensely cold ice age winter arrived, cave bears did what bears that live in northern lands still do today — they went into shelters and hibernated. (Tropical bears do not hibernate.) Cave bears had to fatten up as much as they could during the summer and fall, eating up to 20 hours a day. During the coldest months, they retreated to their caves to hibernate. Cave bears may have slept as long as the current champions, North American black bears, which hibernate for up to 100 days.

When a bear hibernates, its body temperature drops and its breathing slows down. But the bear is really only in a light doze and would wake up if someone blundered into its den.

A bear does not eat or drink during hibernation. All the fat stored up in the summer and fall gradually breaks down, supplying the animal with about 4,000 calories a day. It does not urinate during its long sleep. Instead, its body takes nitrogen from urea — one of the chemicals found in urine — and uses it to build new protein. This protein, along with the stored fat, prevents the hibernating bear from starving.

Even more amazing, female bears give birth during hibernation. Bear cubs are born tiny — only about 1⁄420 of their mother's size. (By comparison, human babies weigh about 1⁄20 as much as their mothers.) The blind babies, almost hairless, instinctively seek out the rich milk from their slumbering mother. It will give the cubs all the nourishment they need until spring.

THE LIFE OF A CAVE BEAR

So many bears padded through the passageways of European caves that the rocks were worn smooth and shiny where their bodies had rubbed. Cave floors and walls became covered with deep scratch marks made by their claws as they walked and stretched. Because of this, and the fact that the bones of so many bears were found together, early researchers once believed that cave bears lived in large groups, unlike any bears today.

However, later scientists realized that the many scratch marks came from a long series of bears using these caves over thousands of years. And if only one cave bear died every other year over a period of 100,000 years, this would account for the bones of approximately 50,000 individual bears found in one cave in Austria. At any one time, a small cave probably held only one female and her cubs, while a larger one might have had space for three or four male bears.

To understand how an animal from prehistoric times once lived, scientists today study the behavior of similar animals alive now. Cave bears, like present-day bears, were most likely solitary animals. Male and female cave bears probably had little to do with each other, except when they mated in the spring. A female bear, however, often had the company of her cubs. The cubs stayed with their fiercely protective mother for two or three years. She taught them how to avoid dangerous places and animals, and where to find food.

Small groups of cave bears that found themselves close together may have behaved the way brown bears do today by developing a social order. The largest adult males would have had the highest ranking, then females with cubs and other adult males. Juvenile bears would have had the lowest ranking. Perhaps male cave bears, like brown bears, generally avoided fighting each other, except when they were competing for mates. Their impressive canine teeth may have been put to good use at those times.

Because of their enormous size, cave bears would have spent a great deal of their time eating and searching for food. Early human beings may have learned what plants were good to eat by watching bears.

A cave bear drags its front claws on the cave wall, perhaps marking its territory, while another bear watches.

CAVE LIFE

True to their name, cave bear remains have almost always been found in caves. Caves would have supplied the bears with shelter from severe weather as well as places to hibernate in winter and give birth to their young. The hilly or mountainous areas in which the caves were located probably provided the ideal environment for the food the bears ate. It is thought that cave bears, unlike modern bears, had a limited range and probably roamed very little from their home base.

Life in a cave was not without its dangers. Some cave bear bones show signs of injuries suffered from accidents that occurred while the bears were in the caves. Pieces of falling rock might damage the bears' skulls and other bones. Other diseases were probably caused by long periods of time spent in cold and damp caves without sunshine. Even the layout of certain caves proved dangerous: in one cave in Germany, several bears fell into a pit and were unable to climb out and died of injuries or starvation.

But most of the remains of cave bears found are of those that died during hibernation. Bears that were old or sick — or hadn't eaten enough to tide them over until spring — never woke up. And their bones were preserved and protected in the caves.

Why did cave bears choose certain caves to live in over others? The cave needed to be deep so that the temperature stayed warm enough for the bears to survive over the winter. Cave bears would also have avoided caves already inhabited by other ferocious predators, especially those that lived in packs like cave lions or hyenas. Once they found the ideal cave, generations of bears would have used it over and over again.

Unexpected meetings between cave bears and human beings must have happened fairly often. They both needed caves for shelter and ate many of the same foods.

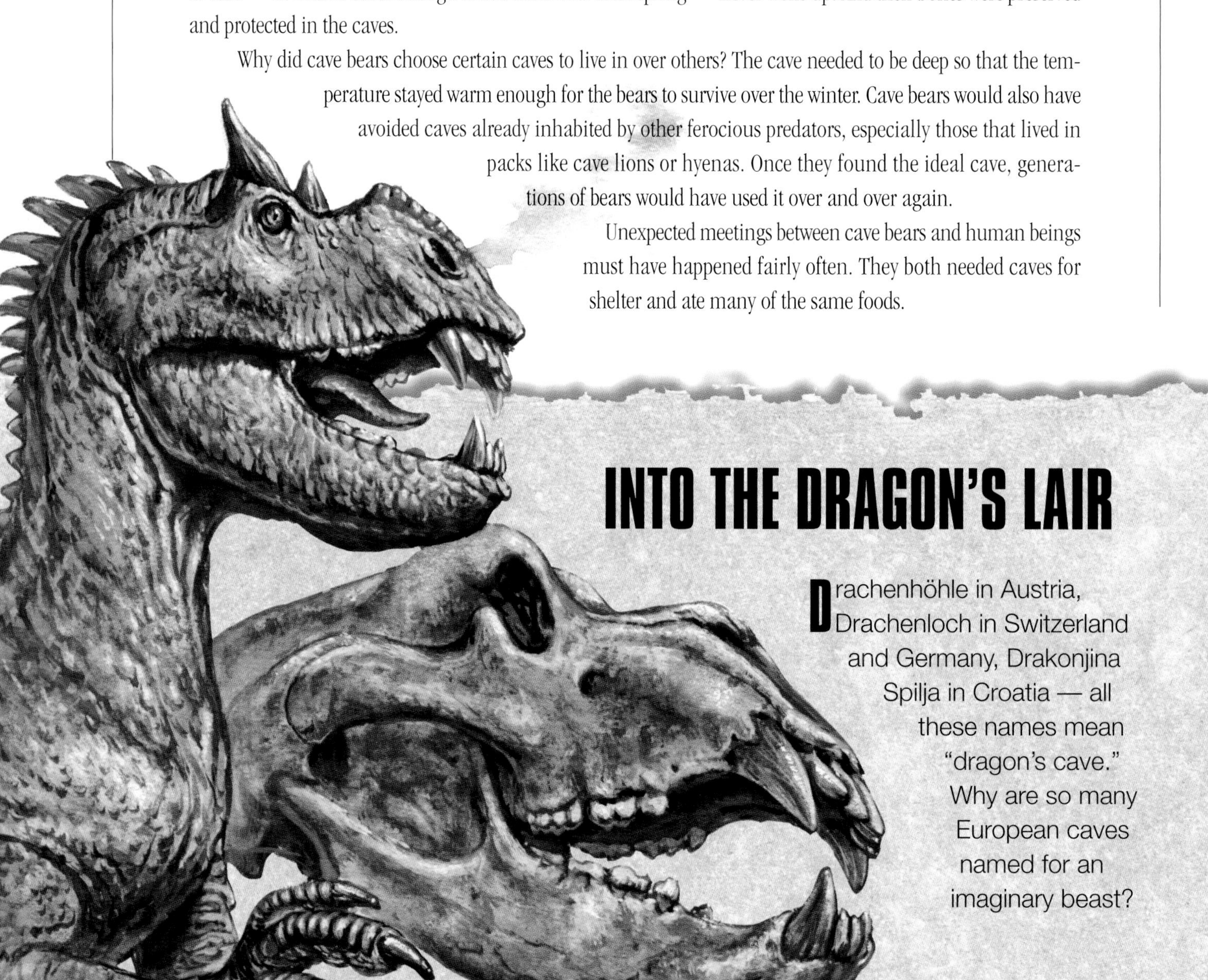

INTO THE DRAGON'S LAIR

Drachenhöhle in Austria, Drachenloch in Switzerland and Germany, Drakonjina Spilja in Croatia — all these names mean "dragon's cave." Why are so many European caves named for an imaginary beast?

The bones of cave bears lie on the floor of the Chauvet Cave (inset), and scratches from their claws still mark the walls (above).

Human beings have always been interested in the fossil remains of ancient creatures. In a cave in Burgundy, France, scientists found a stash of fossils and corals gathered by a prehistoric human some 80,000 years ago — the earliest known "collection." Yet, until about 200 years ago, even educated people did not know what these finds were. The skulls and bones of large extinct animals seemed particularly frightening and many strange tales were invented to explain them.

People who first discovered the huge bones of ice age rhinoceroses, mammoths, and bears in mountain caves believed that giants had roamed the earth. In the Carpathian mountains of eastern Romania, a "dragon's skull" was found in 1672. Fortunately, someone made a drawing of it, and today we can tell that the skull — heavy and long, with large, jutting teeth — actually came from a cave bear. As recently as 1900, the people of Mixnitz, Austria, were still telling tales of a dragon slayer who had rid the countryside of the beasts. The bones of the Mixnitz dragon are really those of a cave bear.

FACE TO FACE WITH CAVE BEARS

The storm struck suddenly, with cold, drenching rain. The man, short but powerfully built, with a heavy, jutting brow, ducked into the mouth of a cave. The woman followed him. They cringed as deafening thunderclaps echoed on the mountainsides and lightning lit up the sky. Then they heard something behind them that terrified them even more — heavy snuffling and the scraping of huge clawed feet moving toward them.

The man and woman backed out of the cave, almost falling, as the angry bear charged. At the cave mouth, the bear reared up on its hind legs and opened its mouth wide, showing long, pointed canines. The desperate man threw his spear at the creature, and then the humans turned and ran for their lives.

Cave bears lived alongside three different human groups in Europe. The first was *Homo heidelbergensis,* an early human being with a powerful build and overhanging brow who lived about 600,000 to 100,000 years ago. (The first cave bears appeared about 300,000 years ago.) Next came the Neanderthals, also stocky and with heavy brows, who lived from 200,000 to 30,000 years ago. Finally, early modern human beings — *Homo sapiens* — arrived in Europe somewhere between 30,000 and 40,000 years ago, probably overlapping with the Neanderthals. All these early humans left some kind of record of their encounters with bears.

Researchers used to think that Homo heidelbergensis did not have the skill to hunt bears or other large animals. Then, in the late 1990s, scientists announced an unusual find in Schoeningen, Germany. They had uncovered throwing spears, made of spruce, that were 400,000 years old — the oldest wooden weapons ever found. Along with the spears, they found the bones of bears and other animals, some with cut marks on them from butchering. Later humans hunted bears, too: at a Neanderthal site in Hungary, researchers found the bones of 500 bears. Homo sapiens, armed with bows and arrows as well as spears, were even better bear hunters.

Evidence of humans hunting cave bears, however, is very rare. Early human beings and cave bears probably avoided each other whenever possible. The bears were enormous and would have been powerful and terrifying opponents. Even large groups of humans would not have attempted to kill a cave bear unless absolutely necessary. Other animals would have been easier to catch for food and less dangerous. Most of the bears hunted by prehistoric people in Europe were the smaller brown bears.

But early humans not only hunted bears, they were fascinated by them. Paintings at the Chauvet Cave and other sites in France show how carefully the artists had looked at bears. A painting from the Trois-Frères Cave shows what looks like a bear wounded by spears, with blood pouring out of its mouth. Was this art meant to have magical powers? Perhaps these long-ago people believed that painting a dangerous animal would help you hunt it or keep it from harming you.

Another piece of bear art from France, even stranger than the cave paintings, also seems to have something to do with hunting. In 1923, near Montespan in the French Pyrénées mountains, a cave explorer found an ancient life-sized model of a massive bear, made from almost 1,500 pounds (680 kg) of clay. The headless sculpture was riddled with spear marks, as if it had been used in a hunting ritual.

(Left) A giant bear startles a Neanderthal family sheltering in its cave.

CAVE BEAR WORSHIP

Did early human beings worship the cave bear? From 1917 to 1921, a scientist explored the Drachenloch cave in Switzerland. He thought that there was something unusual about the placement of cave bear remains he found there. And because Neanderthals had also lived in the cave at one time, he concluded that these prehistoric people must have arranged the cave bear bones and skulls in a specific way for some sort of ceremony. In one case, the leg bone of a cave bear appeared to be deliberately inserted into the cheek-bone of a cave bear skull. Other caves were found with bear bones that also appeared to be deliberately arranged under stone slabs. And in one ancient site, bear bones were found buried with those of human beings. It was not long before the idea that the Neanderthals worshiped cave bears became popular.

But most scientists today do not believe that prehistoric cave bear cults ever existed. They say that arrangements of cave bear bones in many European caves can be explained by natural causes. Flooding in a cave may have caused cave bear skulls and bones to end up pointing in a single direction, or may even have pushed a leg bone through the cheekbone of a skull. The bears that lived in the same cave over a period of several thousand years could have pushed old bones aside into piles when getting ready to hibernate. A cave roof could collapse on top of a number of skeletons, creating the appearance that a rock slab was deliberately placed, forming a cave bear "grave." And finally, Neanderthal people may simply have buried bear remains with those of human beings to keep scavengers away.

Still, the cave bear clearly made a strong impression on the imagination of prehistoric people. At Chauvet, the bears were painted in red on the cave walls over 30,000 years ago by Homo sapiens called Cro-Magnons. Scientists studying Chauvet have found the skulls of at least 147 different cave bears that may have gone into the chambers to hiber-nate and then died there.

Was the Chauvet Cave a spiritual place for ancient people? It is possible that Cro-Magnon hunters found the Chauvet Cave full of cave bear bones and, inspired by the strange atmosphere of the place, began to paint there. Ancient people most commonly painted the largest and most powerful animals that were living at the time. Did they believe this gave them strength during a hunt?

Since Chauvet was first discovered, cave bear bones have been found stuck vertically into the ground in one of the chambers. And what about that bear skull on the stone at Chauvet? Scientists know that the block had fallen quite naturally from the ceiling and was not carved by human hands. But the skull was placed on the stone on purpose. Could it have been part of some prehistoric ritual? This is a puzzle we may never solve.

(Left) A cave bear painting found in the Chauvet Cave. (Top) The rocky hills of the Ardèche region in France, where the Chauvet Cave is located. (Middle) The cave bear skull atop the stone block. (Bottom) An ancient footprint of a boy.

UNCOVERING ANCIENT CLUES

Because of a dispute about ownership of the site, scientists couldn't begin their work at the Chauvet Cave until the spring of 1998. A 12-member core team studies the cave for just two weeks at a time, twice a year. A second team makes only two additional weeklong visits. Specialists in many different fields are looking for clues — traces of pollen, types of charcoal, evidence of past flooding or other changes to the cave's environment. At this slow pace, it will take years to uncover all the possible information. But any more time spent in the cave would threaten the prehistoric art. Just breathing in the enclosed space causes the air to become warm, and mold might begin to grow on the walls, ruining the art. But the experts have already unlocked some of the cave's secrets.

Prehistoric people first began using the cave about 35,000 years ago. At that time, a fire was built on the fallen rock slab on which the cave bear skull was placed. But there are no signs that human beings ever lived in the cave. Scientists have found only traces of animal-fat lamps and torches, fire pits, and the colored powders the artists used. There were no cooking fires or remains of food. A second group of ancient people returned 6,000 years later. It is not known whether they came to view the existing art or to create more. The experts have even found the footprint of an 8-to-10-year-old boy, preserved in what was once the soft clay of the cave floor.

THE WORLD OF THE CAVE BEAR

During the time of the cave bear, many other large animals flourished. The panoramic scene below shows a European mountain valley about 20,000 years ago.

1. A Megaloceros, *a kind of giant deer with antlers as big as 12 feet (3.6 m) across, watches as mammoths feed alongside some much smaller horses.*
2. A Homotherium *(a type of sabertooth cat) looks up from its prey as cave hyenas approach.*
3. *An arctic fox family emerges from their den.*

4. *An angry mother cave bear rears up to protect her cub from a pair of cave lions.*

5. *Lemmings (small rodents) feast on the abundant vegetation of the valley.*

6. *A pair of woolly rhinos fight while some reindeer pass by behind them.*

Most of the larger mammals (*Megaloceros,* mammoths, *Homotherium,* cave bears, cave lions, cave hyenas, woolly rhinos) are now extinct.

A GREAT MIGRATION

During the ice age, cave bears were not the only bears in Europe. Beginning about 250,000 years ago, they shared the landscape with brown bears (*Ursus arctos*). In northern regions, polar bears first appeared about 200,000 years ago. Scientists think that they arose from a group of brown bears that lived along the Arctic coast of Siberia and specialized in hunting seals.

Although cave bears and brown bears had a common ancestor, they lived differently. Brown bears would eat plants and berries, but they also attacked and killed large animals such as reindeer. And while the cave bear remained in Europe, the brown bear spread across Asia and into the New World — without ever getting its paws wet.

During the Pleistocene ice age, so much of the world's water was trapped in glaciers that sea levels were much lower than they are now. Between Siberia and Alaska, where the Bering Sea is today, animals could walk on dry land. This area, known as Beringia, was a broad, grassy plain, dotted with dwarf birch and willow trees, almost three-quarters the size of the United States. Many animals made the journey across Beringia from their old homes in Asia and Europe, including mammoths, sabertooth cats, musk oxen — and brown bears. Human beings also entered North America across the land bridge, probably following the herds of animals they hunted.

Beringia had been reappearing and disappearing for millions of years whenever sea levels rose and fell. When the brown bears arrived in North America, they found a continent already well stocked with bears whose ancestors had made the crossing two or three million years earlier. There were black bears (*Ursus americanus*) and the group of bears called the tremarctines. One of the tremarctines, the Florida cave bear (*Tremarctos floridanus*), lived much the same life as a European cave bear, feeding mostly on plants and living in caves in the southeastern United States and Mexico. But another tremarctine, the giant short-faced bear (*Arctodus simus*), was one of the largest, strongest meat-eating bears the world has ever known.

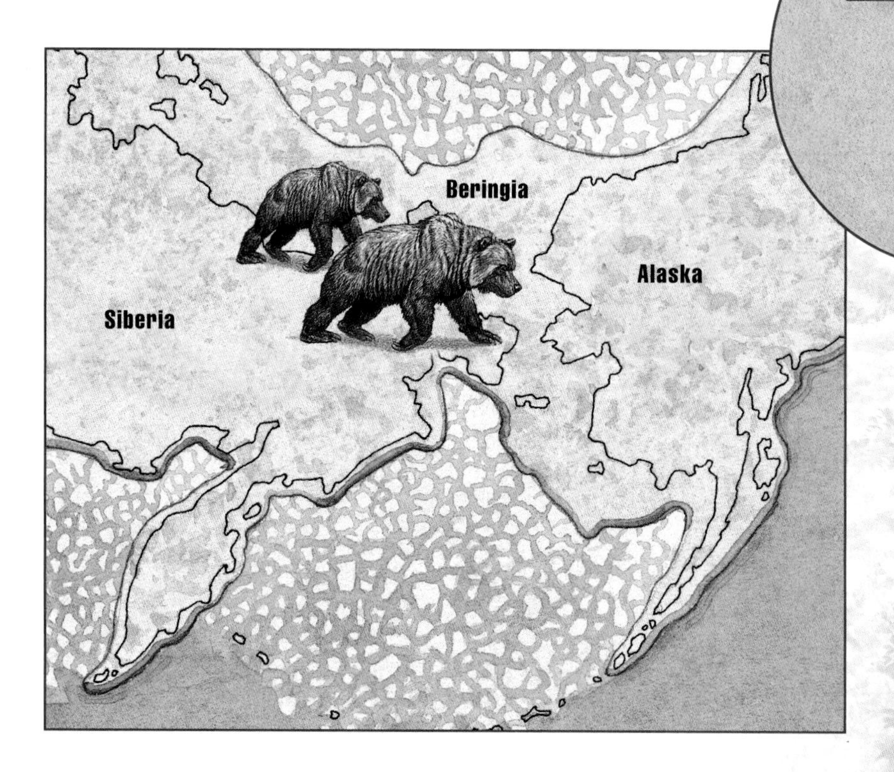

(Left) The Beringia land bridge between Siberia and Alaska. (Above) Beringia. (Right) Two brown bears search for food as they cross to North America.

ANOTHER ICE AGE GIANT

The young mammoth was thirsty and saw water at the bottom of the steep-sided pond. As he drew nearer, its sloping sides crumbled and his feet slid out from under him. He fell into the shallow pool at the bottom with a loud splash. Although he could get to his feet again, he could not get out. Each time he put his front feet on the side of the water hole, more of the earth broke away. The young mammoth struggled, trumpeting in distress — and a huge bear came to investigate the noise. Much more agile than the mammoth, the bear would be able to get down the bank and back out again. The mammoth would make a fine meal. But before the bear could get down to the pond, other members of the mammoth herd arrived. One of them angrily charged the bear. Stunned by a blow from a swinging trunk, the bear tumbled into the pond and drowned.

At least, this is what researchers think might have happened at the Hot Springs Mammoth Site in South Dakota. Since 1974, they have uncovered the remains of 50 mammoths — and one short-faced bear — that died there over 20,000 years ago.

The giant short-faced bear roamed over most of western North America during the Pleistocene, from Alaska and the Yukon down to Mexico. It was about 30 percent bigger than today's brown bear, standing five feet (1.5 m) high at the shoulder when on all fours, and weighing up to 1,500 pounds (680 kg). When it stood upright, it towered some 11 feet (3.4 m) tall. The bear's short muzzle and large, pointed teeth made its head look more like a lion's than that of a bear today. Unlike those of other bears, its feet did not turn in, and its legs were long and lean, so it was probably an excellent runner.

The short-faced bear was the most powerful carnivore in Pleistocene North America, far outweighing the sabertooth cats and American lions of its day. Some scientists believe that the bear was a fierce predator, crushing the spines of bison and musk oxen with one sweep of its mighty paws and piercing their thick hides with its powerful jaws and teeth.

Scientists have been able to analyze the chemical content of short-faced bear bones. Comparing the results with today's carnivores, they have been able to prove that this bear was indeed a meat-eater. However, Paul Matheus, a scientist who has studied the remains of short-faced bears in Alaska, argues that the bears were too large to pursue prey swiftly. Instead, he believes they must have been scavengers. The bears had particularly strong hipbones and probably stood upright often. Matheus thinks they used their height to scan and sniff their surroundings, searching for lions or wolves grouped around their kills. Then the bears would use their great size to intimidate the predators, driving them away and stealing their food.

THE END OF THE LINE

What became of the last cave bear? Did it fall to a hunter's spear? Or did it crawl into a cave, starving and weak, and never wake up from hibernation?

About 10,000 years ago, cave bears became extinct in Europe. Around the same time, North American short-faced bears and Florida cave bears also disappeared forever. Along with them, many other large animals vanished, including cave lions, woolly rhinos, and giant deer in Europe, and sabertooth cats and mammoths in North America. It is puzzling that so many large and powerful animals made it through the harsh conditions of the ice age, only to die when the climate became milder.

Extinction — the death of all members of a plant or animal species — is one of the great mysteries of life on earth. In recent centuries, human beings have caused the disappearance of many creatures, but great extinctions were occurring long before human beings first appeared. Can some of the extinctions of large mammals at the end of the ice age be pinned on our own species?

Some scientists believe we are to blame. Human beings armed with spears and bows and arrows entered North America only a few thousand years before the animals disappeared. They may have overhunted the big game animals. Bears and big cats would have died out soon afterward because their prey was gone.

Other scientists think that changing climate and vegetation killed the ice age giants. As temperature and rainfall changed, different plants replaced the old ones. The plant-eaters would have died when their most nourishing foods disappeared; the meat-eaters would have been left without food when the plant-eaters vanished. Yet another theory is that an unknown deadly disease killed the ice age animals. Some scientists think that the extinction of cave bears was a gradual process that took place over thousands of years.

Many unanswered questions remain. In Europe, unlike North America, early humans and cave bears lived side by side for over 100,000 years before these bears became extinct. Furthermore, why did only cave bears and short-faced bears vanish, while the black, brown, and polar bears survived? Is it possible that these bears slowly pushed out the cave bears and took over their territories?

(Top) A European stone spearhead dating from the time cave bears became extinct. (Above) An ancient artist carved this bear-shaped club out of granite. (Right) A woman scrapes the hide of one of the last cave bears.

BEARS TODAY

Bears were once found in every part of the world except Australia and Antarctica, but only eight species remain today.

In South America, there is just one: the spectacled bear (*Tremarctos ornatus*), the last survivor of the tremarctine group of bears. Named for light-colored rings around its eyes that look like a pair of glasses, this shaggy black bear lives on the slopes of the Andes mountains. Its cloud forest home has been cut down for farms, and now less than 2,000 bears live in the wild.

All four Asian bear species are threatened with extinction, their habitat taken over by humans. But an added threat is that bear organs provide high-priced ingredients for traditional Far Eastern medicines. The sun bear (*Ursus malayanus*) of Southeast Asia is the world's smallest, the size of a Saint Bernard. The Asiatic black bear (*Ursus thibetanus*) resembles the American black bear, except for a V-shaped band of cream-colored fur across its chest. Sloth bears (*Ursus ursinus*) are found in Sri Lanka, India, Bhutan, Nepal, and Bangladesh. They were once mistaken for sloths because of their long fur and large, floppy ears.

Scientists once thought the giant panda (*Ailuropoda melanoleuca*) of China was related to raccoons. But studies of its DNA have shown that it should be grouped with bears. The panda has flexible front paws with a wrist bone that acts like a sixth digit — almost like our thumbs — so that it can strip bamboo leaves, its main food, from the stems. Fewer than 1,000 of these bears remain in the wild.

There are more American black bears (*Ursus americanus*) than any other kind of bear, perhaps as many as

(Opposite) The South American spectacled bear. (Top left) The sun bear. (Top middle) The Asiatic black bear. (Top right) The giant panda. (Bottom) The sloth bear.

700,000. Often confused with brown bears, black bears are a different species. Living in forests from the far northern tree line down to the Sierra Madre mountains of Mexico, they weigh between 130 and 660 pounds (59 and 300 kg). They choose habitats well away from the larger brown bears and eat everything from nuts and berries to creatures as small as ants and as large as a young moose. These bears may be many colors besides black: cinnamon brown, beige — even a bluish gray color. On small islands off the coast of British Columbia, Canada, live the rarest "black" bears of all, the Kermode, or spirit, bears. They are white with brown eyes and black noses.

Brown bears (*Ursus arctos*) are the bears of European fairy tales. In North America, brown bears are also known as grizzly bears. (The name "grizzly" comes from the "grizzled," or silvery, hair tips on some bears.) Brown bears are usually dark brown, but can range from cream-colored to nearly black. The largest brown bears live on Kodiak Island in Alaska and weigh up to 1,500 pounds (680 kg), while some European brown bears weigh as little as 150 pounds (68 kg). A distinctive hump of muscle above their shoulders makes these bears powerful diggers. Although they look slow, brown bears can run as fast as greyhounds, about 40 mph (almost 65 km/h). But they can only maintain that speed for a short distance. Today, only 125,000 to 150,000 brown bears remain in the world, with about a third of these living in western Canada and Alaska.

Polar bears, along with Kodiak bears, are the largest land carnivores on earth. Some weigh over 1,300 pounds (600 kg). They roam the sea ice of the Arctic and the nearby shores of Norway, Siberia, Alaska, Canada, and Greenland. Their Latin name, *Ursus maritimus*, means "sea bear," and polar bears, with their streamlined heads and webbed paws, are excellent swimmers. Unlike other bears, polar bears are almost entirely meat-eaters. Seals are their main prey, and a polar bear can smell one even below three feet (1 m) of ice or snow.

There are 20,000 to 40,000 polar bears still in the wild — 15,000 of them in Canada — and they are protected in all their territories. Only the native peoples of the Arctic, such as the Inuit, are allowed to hunt them. In Inuit legend, *Nanuk,* or the polar bear, is considered to be wise and powerful and to possess a soul. The Labrador Innu believed that a giant polar bear ruled over all the animals and decided whether or not to send whales and seals into open water for hunters to kill.

AN AGE-OLD FASCINATION

For as long as people could record their thoughts and feelings, and probably long before that, they have been fascinated by bears. Bears are large and powerful animals, yet they seem similar to human beings in many ways. Their broad foreheads have struck many people as intelligent-looking. Like human beings, bears can stand upright, and their feet leave human-like tracks on the ground. Like us, they are playful and curious, and like us, they eat everything from meat to berries, nuts, and honey. Mother bears have long been admired for the care and protection they give their cubs.

Ancient peoples all over the world looked up at the night sky and saw the outline of a bear prowling among the stars. Even today, that group of stars, or constellation, is known as Ursa Major, the Great Bear, while another constellation nearby is called Ursa Minor, the Little Bear.

We cannot reach back in time to understand what prehistoric people felt when they painted a cave bear or placed its skull on a stone platform. But we know that they lived close to bears and truly knew how they lived, in a way that few people today can imagine. Perhaps the closest we can come to understanding this vanished ice age relationship is to look at the traditional beliefs of North America's native people and other aboriginal peoples who have also known and respected bears.

Because hibernating bears seemed to die and miraculously come back to life, bears were often considered great healers. Among the people of the Great Plains, nothing was stronger than a grizzly-hide medicine bundle, a pouch believed to have special powers. The Nani people of Siberia, the Ainu of northern Japan, and the Modoc of the Pacific Northwest believed that bears — who once walked upright and spoke — were their ancestors.

European settlers who came to North America competed with bears for food and space. That competition still goes on today. Bears are large and can be dangerous — but bear attacks that kill people are unusual, far rarer than fatal attacks by domestic dogs, or even bees. Today, it is bears who are in danger from human beings. We give them too little space and lure them too close with the smells from camping food or garbage bins. Bears today need the same things the cave bears needed — shelter and space to roam, find food, and raise their young. It is in our hands whether they will continue to find it.

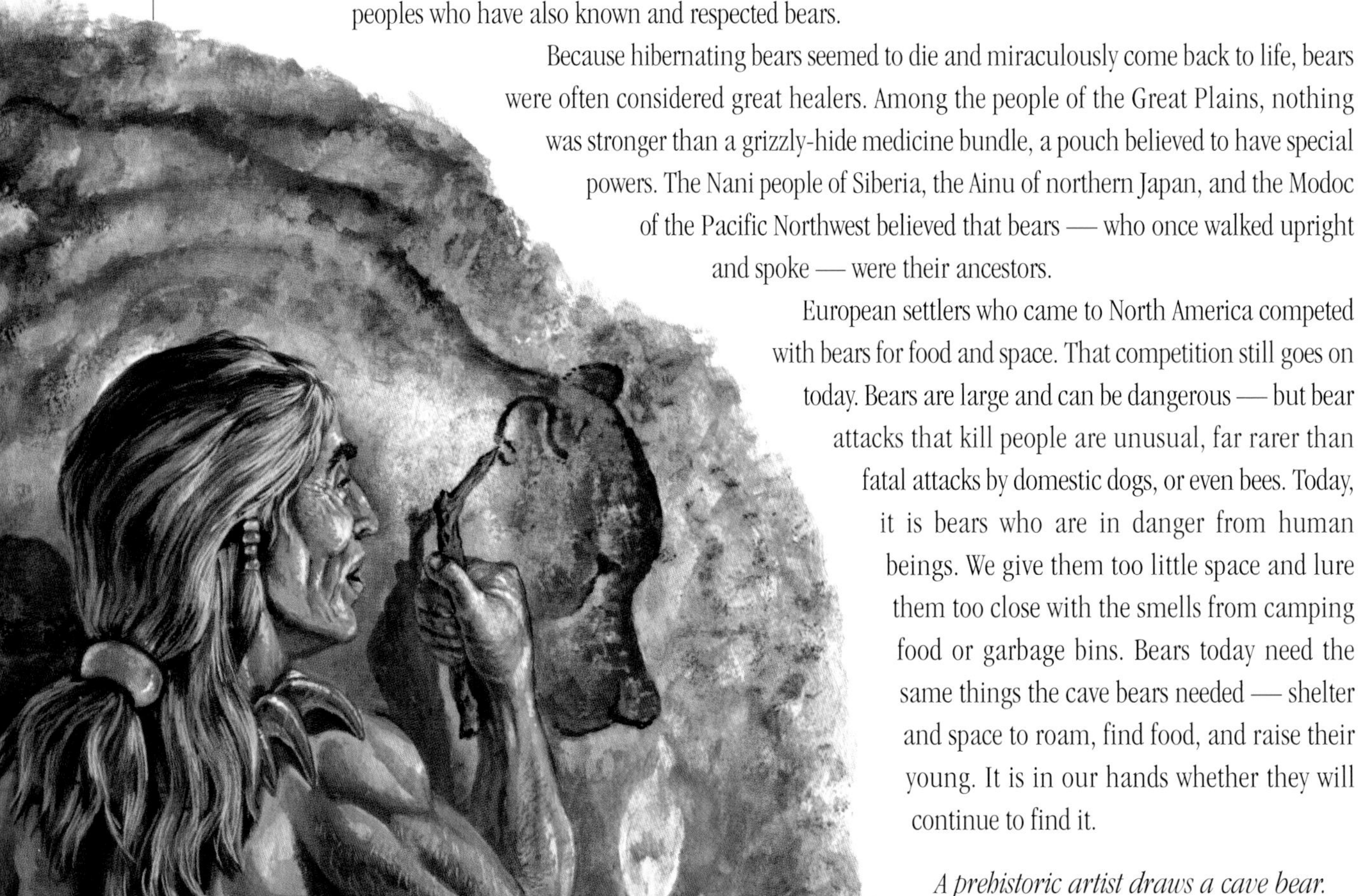

A prehistoric artist draws a cave bear.

GLOSSARY

cult: A system of worship based on ritual.

DNA: The abbreviation for deoxyribonucleic acid, a complex chemical compound found in cells that carries hereditary information.

fossil: Preserved remains of a plant or animal that lived in prehistoric times.

habitat: The place or environment where a plant or animal normally lives.

muzzle: The projecting jaws and snout of an animal.

nitrogen: A colorless and odorless gas that is the most plentiful element in the earth's atmosphere and a part of all living matter.

Pleistocene Epoch: The period from approximately 1.7 million to 10,000 years ago, marked by great changes in temperature and sheets of ice advancing and retreating across the earth.

predator: A creature that hunts and kills other animals for food.

protein: A complex substance, of great nutritional value, found in all living things.

ritual: A ceremony performed as part of a system of religious beliefs.

scavenger: A creature that feeds on the remains of dead animals.

species: A single kind of plant or animal.

subarctic tundra: A treeless plain covered in moss and low shrubs, found just outside the arctic region.

subtropical forest: A wooded area found just outside the tropics, the region around the equator.

tuber: A fleshy underground stem with tiny buds capable of producing a new plant.

RECOMMENDED FURTHER READING

For young readers:

Bears and Pandas by Michael Bright. Lorenz Books.
Full of fascinating information, this book will interest 8-to-12-year olds.

For older readers:

Bear: A Celebration of Power and Beauty by Rebecca Grambo, photographs by Daniel J. Cox. Sierra Club.
This beautiful book looks at bears and their long relationship with human beings.

Dawn of Art: The Chauvet Cave by Jean-Marie Chauvet, Eliette Brunel Deschamps, and Christian Hillaire. Harry N. Abrams, Inc.
The stunning photos taken inside Chauvet reveal the skill and imagination of Cro-Magnon artists.

WEB SITES

www.bearden.org/index.html
This web site put together by the American Zoo and Aquarium Association presents lots of information on modern bears as well as some fun games.

www.culture.gouv.fr/culture/arcnat/chauvet/en/
The official web site for the Chauvet Cave allows you to virtually explore the cave, chamber by chamber.

PICTURE CREDITS

All illustrations are by Mark Hallett unless otherwise stated.

4: Courtesy of The Stone Company, Boulder, Colorado

5: (Right) Image no. 5270(2), photo by D. Finnin and J. Beckett, American Museum of Natural History Library; (inset) Jean Clottes, French sub-direction of archaeology, French Ministry of Culture and Communication.

10: Map by Jack McMaster.

15: (Top and inset) Courtesy of Jean Clottes.

18: French Ministry of Culture and Communication, Regional Direction for Cultural Affairs, Rhône-Alpes region, Regional department of archaeology.

19: (Top) French Ministry of Culture and Communication, Regional Direction for Cultural Affairs, Rhône-Alpes region, Regional preservation of ancient monuments; (middle) courtesy of Jean Clottes; (bottom) Michel-Alain Garcia, CNRS-MAE Nanterre.

22: Maps by Jack McMaster.

26: (Top and bottom) C.M. Dixon.

28: Kevin Schafer, NHPA.

29: (Top left and top middle) Andy Rouse, NHPA; (top right and bottom) James Warwick, NHPA.

INDEX

ACKNOWLEDGMENTS

Many thanks to Hugh Brewster for encouraging me to create an Ice Age series and for his keen interest in the books as they have progressed. Thanks also to Bruce McLellan, who kindly provided me with a copy of his clear and succinct paper, co-authored with David C. Reiner, on bear evolution. And, as always, thank you to my editor, Susan Aihoshi, who tirelessly tracked down obscure facts and found the perfect photographs to illustrate the text. — *Barbara Hehner*

This book is for my dear wife Turi, whose supportiveness and patience with the life of an artist make it possible for me to achieve all things. — *Mark Hallett*

Madison Press Books would like to thank our scientific consultants at the Royal Ontario Museum, Dr. Mark Engstrom, director of research and senior curator of mammals in the Centre for Biodiversity and Conservation Biology, and Dr. Kevin Seymour, assistant curator of Palaeobiology; Florence Magovern of The Stone Company, Boulder, Colorado; Matt Pavlick of the American Museum of Natural History, New York; Dr. Aurora Grandal d'Anglade of the University of Coruña, Spain; Paul Mazza of the Museum of Natural History, Florence, Italy; and the French Ministry of Culture and Communication, Regional Direction for Cultural Affairs, Rhône-Alpes, Regional Department of Archaeology, Lyon, France. Special thanks are extended to Dr. Jean Clottes, director of the Chauvet Cave research team.

First published by
Crown Publishers, a division of
Random House, Inc.
1540 Broadway,
New York, New York 10036

CROWN and colophon are trademarks of
Random House, Inc.

www.randomhouse.com/kids

Library of Congress
Cataloging-in-Publication Data

Hehner, Barbara.
Ice Age cave bear : the giant beast that terrified ancient humans / by Barbara Hehner; illustrations by Mark Hallett; scientific consultation by Mark Engstrom and Kevin Seymour. — 1st ed.
p. cm.
Includes bibliographical references and index.
Summary: Describes how and where cave bears lived, possible reasons for their extinction, and what kind of relationship might have existed between these huge creatures and prehistoric man.
ISBN 0-375-81329-2 (trade)
ISBN 0-375-91329-7 (lib. bdg.)
1. Cave bear—Juvenile literature.
[1. Cave bear. 2. Bears. 3. Mammals, Fossil. 4. Prehistoric animals. 5. Human-animal relationships.] I. Hallett, Mark, 1947– ill.
II. Title.
QE882.C15 H43 2002
569'.78—dc21 2001052953

Printed in Singapore

October 2002

10 9 8 7 6 5 4 3 2 1

Editorial Director: Hugh Brewster
Art Director: Gordon Sibley
Project Editor: Susan Aihoshi
Editorial Assistance: Lloyd Davis, Nan Froman
Production Director: Susan Barrable
Production Manager: Donna Chong
Color Separation: Colour Technologies
Printing and Binding: Imago Productions, Singapore

ICE AGE CAVE BEAR
was produced by
Madison Press Books,
which is under the direction of
Albert E. Cummings

Madison Press Books
1000 Yonge Street, Suite 200
Toronto, Ontario
Canada
M4W 2K2